Cooking Ideas for Brie Cheese

The Diverse Features of Brie: A Tasty Portrait

The Ultimate Cheese Recipes We Love

By

Rola Oliver

License Notice

Table of Contents

Introduction 5

1. Chicken pancetta in cream sauce 6

2. Baked Brie with Onions 9

3. Cranberry and Brie Pizza 11

4. Baked Chicken with Brie sauce 13

5. Baked Brie Chutney 15

6. Brie with Figs and Toasted almonds 17

7. Basil Brie Fettuccini 19

8. Marinara with Brie 21

9. Brie Fondue 23

10. Apple Cinnamon Grilled Cheese 25

11. Baked Brie 27

12. Oyster Crostini 29

13. Brie cups 31

14. Brie Quesadillas with Pear 33

15. Brie and Prosciutto Chicken 35

16. Brie chicken with raspberry sauce and pecans 37

17. Bruschetta Dip 40

18. Brie and Mango salmon 42

19. Pear and Walnut Flatbread 44

20. Brie Mac and Cheese 47

21. Caramel apple Brie Bites 50

22. Brie on a baguette with pear and black pepper 52

23. Grilled Pear and Brie Sandwich 54

24. Honey Brie spread 56

25. Brie Pizza 58

26. Bacon Brie Panini 60

27. Brie Asparagus Casserole 62

28. Spinach and Brie Linguine 64

29. Chicken Wellington with Brie 66

30. Brie Pasta 68

Author's Afterthoughts 70

About the Author 71

Introduction

Looking for some new and exciting ways to use your brie cheese? Look no further! These cooking ideas will have you whipping up some delicious dishes in no time at all. From simple grilled cheese sandwiches to more complex recipes like quiche, there's something for everyone on this list. Each of the meals in *"Cooking Ideas for Brie Cheese - The Diverse Features of Brie: A Tasty Portrait"* is simple to create, and most need no more than five to thirty minutes of prep work. The holidays are a great opportunity to explore your inner creativity and learn about unusual wines and liquors that go well with this tasty dairy product. Every year, as the calendar winds down, liquor retailers introduce limited-edition holiday-themed beer, wine, and champagne blends. These party beverages are always a hit with guests and can be purchased for a reasonable price.

wwwwwwwwwwwwwwwwwwwwwwwwwwwwwwwww

1. Chicken pancetta in cream sauce

Cooking Time: 45 minutes

Makes:4

Ingredient List:

- 2 ounces extra-virgin olive oil
- 40 ounces chicken breast cutlets, pounded
- 8 ounces of all-purpose flour
- 4 chopped cloves of garlic
- 1 chopped shallot
- 1 ½ ounces sun-dried tomatoes, oil-packed & chopped
- 3 finely chopped slices of pancetta bacon
- 6 ounces dry sherry wine
- 4 ounces of chicken stock
- 2 egg yolks
- 4 ounces heavy cream
- 1-ounce room temperature Brie cheese with rind removed
- A pinch of salt and pepper
- 1 tsp. parsley, chopped

How to Cook:

i. Heat oil in a large frying on medium-high heat

ii. Put flour on a plate. Roll the chicken in the flour, shake off excess and then place the chicken in the heated oil

iii. Fry meat until browned on each side and remove. Set aside

iv. Mix garlic, shallot, tomatoes, and pancetta in the same frying pan and turn the heat down to medium

v. Cook for 2 minutes, stirring constantly until the pancetta is completely cooked

vi. Add sherry to the pan and simmer until half the liquid has evaporated

vii. Add chicken stock and again simmer until half the liquid is gone

viii. In a small bowl, whisk egg and cream, then add to the frying pan

ix. Sprinkle with salt and pepper and transfer chicken to the frying pan mixture

x. Cook all Ingredient List: for 2 minutes or until sauce is thick and has completely coated chicken

xi. Add Brie and mix until smooth

xii. Serve with a sprinkle of chopped parsley

2. Baked Brie with Onions

Cooking Time: 15 minutes

Makes: 8

Ingredient List:

- 1 garlic bulb
- 2 ounces butter
- 1 sliced yellow onion
- 1 peeled Granny Smith apple, cored and sliced
- 8 ounces of Brie cheese
- 1 thawed sheet of frozen puff pastry
- ½ ounce butter, melted

wwwwwwwwwwwwwwwwwwwwwwwwwwwwwwwwww

How to Cook:

i. Preheat oven to 400°F.

ii. Put the garlic bulb on a baking sheet and drizzle with oil

iii. Roast in the oven for 20 minutes or until soft

iv. Remove from oven and set aside

v. Melt 2 ounces of butter in a frying pan on medium heat

vi. Sautee onion and apple in the butter until the apple is tender and the onion is translucent

vii. On a separate baking dish, lay the puff pastry out and place the brie on top

viii. Layer the apple and onion on top of the cheese, fold the pastry and seal the edges by pinching them with your fingers

ix. Brush the pastry with the melted butter and place the dish in the oven

x. Place garlic on a baking sheet, and drizzle with olive oil. Roast for 15 to 20 minutes, or until soft. Set aside.

xi. Bake for 25 minutes or until golden brown

3. Cranberry and Brie Pizza

Cooking Time: 20 minutes

Makes: 4

Ingredient List:

- 16 ounces boneless and skinless chicken breast halves, chopped into small pieces
- ½ ounce vegetable oil
- 12" prepared pizza crust
- 12 ounces cranberry sauce
- 6 ounces chopped Brie
- 8 ounces of mozzarella cheese, shredded

wwwwwwwwwwwwwwwwwwwwwwwwwwwwwwwwwww

How to Cook:

i. Preheat oven to 350°F.

ii. Heat oil in a frying pan on Medium heat and add the chicken and then cook until browned and no longer pink inside

iii. Spread cranberry on the pizza crust on a separate baking sheet. Cover with a layer of chicken, then brie, and then mozzarella.

iv. Bake for 20 minutes or until cheese bubbles and the edges of the crust are golden brown

4. Baked Chicken with Brie sauce

Cooking Time: 5 minutes

Makes:4

Ingredient List:

- 8 ounces of dry white wine
- 32 ounces boneless and skinless chicken breast halves
- A pinch of salt and black pepper
- 1 tsp. oregano, dried
- 8-ounce wheel of Brie cheese

wwwwwwwwwwwwwwwwwwwwwwwwwwwwwwwwwwww

How to Cook:

i.   Preheat the oven to 400°F.

ii. Add wine to a large glass baking dish

iii. Sprinkle salt, pepper, and oregano over the chicken breasts and place them in the dish in one layer

iv. Bake for 40 minutes or until juices run clear

v.   In the meantime, slice the Brie into thick slices about ¼ " thick

vi. Put slices on top of the chicken when it finishes cooking and then put it back in the oven for 5 minutes or until the cheese melts

vii. Serve hot

5. Baked Brie Chutney

Cooking Time: 10 minutes

Makes: 32

Ingredient List:

- 32-ounce wheel of Brie cheese
- 1/3 ounce curry powder, ground
- 12 ounces mango chutney
- 8 ounces cashews, chopped
- 1 sliced French baguette, ½" wide

wwwwwwwwwwwwwwwwwwwwwwwwwwwwwwwwww

How to Cook:

i.   Preheat oven to 350°F.

ii. Rub curry powder over the entire wheel of Brie so that the rind is completely coated

iii. Put the cheese wheel on a large baking dish and top it with a thick layer of chutney then cashews

iv. Bake for 15 minutes or until the cheese is melted and the cashews are golden

v.   Serve with baguette

6. Brie with Figs and Toasted almonds

Cooking Time: 10 minutes

Makes: 12

Ingredient List:

- 4 ounces brown sugar
- 1-ounce water
- 6 fresh figs with stems removed and cut into quarters
- 14-ounce wheel of Brie cheese
- 4 ounces almonds, toasted
- 1/2 tsp. vanilla extract

wwwwwwwwwwwwwwwwwwwwwwwwwwwwwwwww

How to Cook:

i. Preheat oven to 325°F.

ii. In a small saucepan on medium heat, cook sugar and water until sugar is entirely dissolved

iii. Stir in figs and half of the vanilla and cook for 10 minutes or until figs are soft

iv. Add almonds and the other half of the vanilla and stir

v. Put the Brie on a baking sheet and pour the mixture from the saucepan over top

vi. Bake for 15 minutes or until soft. Remove just before it melts

7. Basil Brie Fettuccini

Cooking Time: 25 minutes

Makes: 8

Ingredient List:

- 12 ounces of uncooked fettuccine
- 4 seeded tomatoes, chopped
- 2 minced cloves garlic
- 12 ounces Brie cheese, cubed
- 6 ounces fresh basil, chopped
- 4 ounces olive oil
- ½ ounce red wine vinegar
- 1/2 tsp. salt
- 1/2 tsp. black pepper, ground
- 1 ounce Parmesan cheese, grated

wwwwwwwwwwwwwwwwwwwwwwwwwwwwwwwwwwwwww

How to Cook:

i. Combine tomatoes, garlic, brie cheese, basil, oil, vinegar, salt, and pepper in a large bowl and mix thoroughly

ii. Cover the bowl with some plastic wrap and set aside for 2 hours to marinate at room temperature

iii. Boil Fettucine noodles in a large pot of salted water for 12 minutes or until al dente

iv. Drain the noodles and add to the bowl of sauce. Toss until completely coated and serve on plates or bowls with Parmesan cheese

8. Marinara with Brie

Cooking Time: 5 minutes

Makes: 4

Ingredient List:

- ½ ounce olive oil
- 6 minced cloves garlic
- 32 ounces chopped plum tomatoes
- 4 ounces basil, chopped
- 8 ounces Brie

wwwwwwwwwwwwwwwwwwwwwwwwwwwwwwwww

How to Cook:

i. Heat oil in a large frying pan on medium heat

ii. Add garlic to the oil and cook just before it turns brown

iii. Stir in tomatoes and 2 ounces of basil

iv. Reduce the heat to Low and let the mixture simmer for 45 minutes

v. Remove the rind from the Brie and add it to the pan along with the rest of the basil

vi. Let the cheese melt on its own, then stir constantly to prevent burning

vii. Serve hot over pasta noodles

9. Brie Fondue

Cooking Time: 20 minutes

Makes:4

Ingredient List:

- 2 crushed cloves of garlic
- 8 ounces of dry white wine
- 2 ounces sherry
- 16 ounces cubed Brie cheese, with rind removed
- ½ ounce cornstarch
- A pinch of nutmeg, grated
- A pinch of salt and white pepper

wwwwwwwwwwwwwwwwwwwwwwwwwwwwwwwwwwwww

How to Cook:

i. Take the garlic and rub it along the inside of the fondue pot

ii. Place any extra pieces of garlic along the bottom

iii. Add sherry and wine and turn the heat to medium-low

iv. Coat the brie in cornstarch and add to the fondue pot when the wine is hot

v. Whisk the mixture together and stir often to prevent burning

vi. Remove the pot from the heat and add nutmeg, salt, and pepper

vii. Add more cheese if the fondue appears runny

10. Apple Cinnamon Grilled Cheese

Cooking Time: 15 minutes

Makes: 2

Ingredient List:

- 2 large cinnamon buns like the ones at Cinnabon
- 4 slices old Cheddar, divided
- 4 slices Brie, divided
- 4 slices shredded ham, divided
- 1 peeled and cored apple, sliced and divided
- 1-ounce butter
- 2 large eggs
- 2 ounces milk

wwwwwwwwwwwwwwwwwwwwwwwwwwwwwwwwwww

How to Cook:

i.   Slice the cinnamon buns in half and place them on a flat surface

ii. Place 1 slice of cheddar cheese, followed by Brie, apple, and ham, then another slice of Brie, Cheddar and put the top of the bun back on

iii. Repeat for the other cinnamon bun

iv. Heat the butter in a medium frying pan on medium heat

v.   While the butter is heating up, mix eggs and milk together in a small bowl and dip the sandwiches into the milk mixture before putting them in the pan

vi. Fry the sandwiches for 2 minutes per side or until the cheese is melted and they are golden brown

11. Baked Brie

Cooking Time: 5 minutes

Makes: 8

Ingredient List:

- Cooking spray
- 8 ½ ounces thawed frozen puff pastry
- 8-ounce wheel of Brie
- 2 ounces almonds, sliced

wwwwwwwwwwwwwwwwwwwwwwwwwwwwwwwwwwwwww

How to Cook:

i. Preheat oven to 350°F.

ii. Coat a 9" pan lightly with cooking spray.

iii. Slice the Brie along the center of the wheel so you have two round pieces of Brie with the rind on one side of each

iv. Put the pastry in the center of the pie pan and lay the Brie on top of it with the rind facing down

v. Evenly distribute almonds on top of the Brie and then place the other side of the cheese wheel on the almonds with the rind facing up

vi. Fold the puffed pastry around the cheese and seal the edges

vii. Bake for 20 minutes. Let the Brie cool for a few minutes before serving

12. Oyster Crostini

Cooking Time: 10 minutes

Makes: 12

Ingredient List:

- 1 French baguette
- 1-ounce extra-virgin olive oil
- 12 ounces Brie cheese
- 24 shucked oysters, rinsed and drained
- 2 ounces melted butter
- A pinch of salt and pepper
- 1 seeded red bell pepper, sliced thinly into strips

wwwwwwwwwwwwwwwwwwwwwwwwwwwwwwwwwwww

How to Cook:

i. Preheat oven to 350°F.

ii. Cut the baguette into 24 slices

iii. Brush each piece of bread with olive oil and line it up on a baking sheet

iv. Toast the baguette pieces in the oven for 8 minutes

v. Slice the Brie into 24 pieces of equal proportion

vi. Remove the baguette from the oven and put one slice of Brie on each round piece of bread

vii. Put the baking sheet back in the oven for 5 minutes or until the cheese is melted

viii. Get the baking sheet out of the oven and set it to broil

ix. In a casserole dish, mix oysters, butter, and any leftover salt, pepper, and oil

x. Put the oysters in the broiler and cook for 5 minutes or until the edges start to curl

xi. Remove the dish and put one oyster on top of each crostini garnished with red pepper

13. Brie cups

Cooking Time: 10 minutes

Makes: 15

Ingredient List:

- 8 ounces cubed Brie cheese with rind removed
- 15 phyllo tart cups, frozen
- 4 ounces of raspberry preserves

wwwwwwwwwwwwwwwwwwwwwwwwwwwwwwwwwwwww

How to Cook:

i. Preheat oven to 350°F.

ii. Line a cookie sheet with parchment

iii. Place phyllo cups on the sheet in one layer and put two cubes of Brie in each cup or more until all the Brie is used

iv. Spoon some raspberry preserve over top and bake in the oven for 7 minutes or until the cheese has melted

14. Brie Quesadillas with Pear

Cooking Time: 10 minutes

Makes: 4

Ingredient List:

- 2 x 10''' flour tortillas
- 2 ounces sliced Brie cheese
- 1/2 cored pear, thinly sliced
- A pinch of nutmeg, ground
- A pinch of salt

wwwwwwwwwwwwwwwwwwwwwwwwwwwwwwwwwww

How to Cook:

i.   Spread Brie slices on one tortilla, then the pear slices

ii.   Season with salt and nutmeg

iii.   Place the second tortilla over top of the pears

iv.   Coat a frying pan with cooking spray and cook the quesadilla in the pan on Medium heat for 3 minutes per side or until the cheese melts

v.   Remove the quesadilla from the pan and place it on the serving dish. Cut into wedges and serve

15. Brie and Prosciutto Chicken

Cooking Time: 15 minutes

Makes:2

Ingredient List:

- Cooking spray
- 10 ounces boneless and skinless chicken breast halves
- Half of fresh lemon, cut into 2 wedges
- A pinch of ground pepper
- A pinch of chipotle powder
- 2 slices Brie, ½ " thick
- 1-ounce chives, chopped
- 6 slices prosciutto

wwwwwwwwwwwwwwwwwwwwwwwwwwwwwwwwwwww

How to Cook:

i. Preheat oven to 400°F.

ii. Coat a baking dish with cooking spray

iii. Cut chicken breast in half horizontally and open them up

iv. Sprinkle lemon juice, pepper, and chipotle powder on each side.

v. Add a slice of cheese and some chives inside the chicken and then fold the breasts back together

vi. Take 3 slices of prosciutto and place them side by side, overlapping each on top of the other

vii. Put the stuffed chicken on the bottom edge of the prosciutto and roll it so that the chicken breast is upside down

viii. Tuck in the sides and roll some more until the chicken is completely covered and you reach the end of the prosciutto

ix. With the seam of the rolled prosciutto facing down, place the chicken in the baking dish and bake for 40 minutes or until the juices run clear

16. Brie chicken with raspberry sauce and pecans

Cooking Time: 30 minutes

Makes: 6

Ingredient List:

- 48 ounces of boneless and skinless chicken breast halves, pounded
- 16 ounces of Brie cheese
- 8 ounces green onion, chopped
- 2 crushed cloves of garlic
- 16 ounces toasted pecans, finely chopped
- 1 beaten egg
- 2 ounces water
- 16 ounces fresh raspberries
- 2 ounces white sugar
- 2 ounces water
- A pinch of salt and pepper
- 4 ounces olive oil

How to Cook:

i.   Put the brie into the microwave for 30 seconds to a minute until softened

ii.   Combine brie, onion, and garlic in a large bowl and mix thoroughly

iii.   Spread 2 ounces of the brie mixture on each chicken breast half, roll them up and secure each with a toothpick. Put them on a plate and set them aside

iv.   Add egg and water in a shallow bowl and whisk together

v.   Make a dredging station by having the egg in one bowl, and the toasted pecans in another

vi.   Next, you will need to warm up the oil in a large frying pan on medium-high

vii.   Soak the chicken fully in the egg mixture and then the pecans. Place in the heated oil for 15 minutes, turning to brown on both sides, until the juices run clear

viii.   Mix raspberries, sugar, and water in the blender for 4 minutes and strain in a sieve to remove seeds

ix.   Put the chicken on a paper towel once it has been cooked in the frying pan to drain excess grease

x.   Place chicken on a serving dish and drizzle with the raspberry sauce before serving

17. Bruschetta Dip

Cooking Time: 10 minutes

Makes: 8

Ingredient List:

- 2 chopped plum tomatoes
- 1 chopped onion
- 1 peeled clove garlic, minced
- 1 tsp. basil, chopped
- 1 tsp. parsley, chopped
- 2 ounces olive oil
- 8-ounce wheel of Brie

wwwwwwwwwwwwwwwwwwwwwwwwwwwwwwwwwww

How to Cook:

i. Combine tomatoes, onion, garlic, basil, parsley, and oil in a small bowl, cover tightly with plastic wrap, and chill in the refrigerator for 1-2 hours

ii. Remove the rind from the brie and put it in the microwave for 30 seconds or until the cheese softens a little bit

iii. Take the tomato mixture out of the refrigerator and spoon over the cheese

iv. Put the brie back in the microwave for 1 minute or until the cheese is slightly melted

v. Serve and enjoy

18. Brie and Mango salmon

Cooking Time: 15 minutes

Makes: 4

Ingredient List:

- 1-ounce extra-virgin olive oil
- 4 x 4-ounce salmon fillets
- 4 ounces of sliced Brie
- 1 tsp. butter
- 2 peeled mangos – seeded and diced

wwwwwwwwwwwwwwwwwwwwwwwwwwwwwwwwww

How to Cook:

i. Preheat oven to 350°F.

ii. Heat oil in an oven-safe frying pan on medium heat

iii. Sear each side of the salmon for 4 minutes

iv. Cut Brie into cubes and put them on top of the salmon. Cover the pan and bake for 15 minutes or until salmon is soft enough to flake easily

v. Pour the mango sauce over the salmon and serve

19. Pear and Walnut Flatbread

Cooking Time: 30 minutes

Makes: 12

Ingredient List:

- 10 ounces of prepared pizza dough
- All-purpose flour for dusting
- ½ ounce extra-virgin olive oil
- 8-ounce wheel Brie, sliced into thin pieces
- 6 ounces toasted walnuts, coarsely chopped and divided
- 2 ounces ham, thinly sliced
- A pinch of rosemary
- ½ ounce balsamic vinegar
- ½ ounce honey
- 16 ounces baby arugula
- 1 cored ripe pear, chopped into small pieces

How to Cook:

i. Preheat oven to 450°F.

ii. Line two cookie sheets with parchment paper

iii. Cut pizza dough into two even pieces and roll them out on a flat surface lightly dusted with flour, transfer them to the baking sheets

iv. Brush the crusts with oil, then place pieces of Brie evenly over top both pizza crusts

v. Take half the walnuts and sprinkle over the Brie for both

vi. Cut ham into small pieces and spread over the top of the cheese with some rosemary do the same for the 2nd baking sheet

vii. Put both baking sheets in the oven and bake for 15 minutes

viii. Stir balsamic and honey together in a bowl, then add pear, arugula, and the rest of the walnuts

ix. Remove the crusts from the oven and spread the walnut mixture over them evenly

x. Cut into small squares and serve

20. Brie Mac and Cheese

Cooking Time: 25 minutes

Makes: 4

Ingredient List:

- 1 ounce dried shiitake mushrooms
- 8 ounces small shell pasta
- 2 ounces butter, unsalted
- 1 finely chopped leek
- 1 finely chopped shallot
- 2 ounces of all-purpose flour
- 1 tsp. Worcestershire sauce
- 1/8 tsp. black pepper, ground
- 8 ounces of warmed milk
- 1 chopped tomato
- 2 tofu wieners, cut into thick slices
- 6 ounces of Cheddar cheese, grated
- 3 ounces Brie cheese, with rind removed
- 2 ounces of Asiago cheese, grated
- 2 ounces milk
- 5 ½ ounces bread crumbs
- 1 tsp. paprika, ground

How to Cook:

i. Preheat oven to 425°F.

ii. Cover mushrooms with warm water in a small bowl and let them soak for 30 minutes

iii. Drain in a colander and chop, set aside

iv. Cut Brie cheese into cubes and set aside

v. Boil salted water in a large pot, then add pasta noodles

vi. Cook for 8 minutes or until al dente. Drain and set aside.

vii. In a large stockpot, melt butter on medium heat

viii. Stir leeks and shallot into the butter for 2 minutes or until tender

ix. Reduce heat to Low and add flour, Worcestershire sauce, and pepper. Whisk Ingredient List: together

x. Slowly pour in the milk, constantly stirring, until combined with the rest of the mixture in the stockpot

xi. Simmer on Low for 5 minutes

xii. Add mushrooms, tomato, and wieners to the sauce in the pot and fold the pasta in gently

xiii. Add all of the cheeses, stirring constantly until melted

xiv. Pour the entire mixture from the stockpot into a casserole dish. Add some milk if it is too thick

xv. Sprinkle breadcrumbs and paprika over the top, cover, and bake for 20 minutes

21. Caramel apple Brie Bites

Cooking Time: 15 minutes

Makes: 5

Ingredient List:

- 7" wheel of Brie
- 2 peeled and cored Granny Smith apples, diced
- ½ ounce butter
- 1-ounce brown sugar
- ½ ounce caramel sauce
- 7 ounces of pretzel crisps, made by Snack Factory

wwwwwwwwwwwwwwwwwwwwwwwwwwwwwwwwwwwww

How to Cook:

i. Preheat oven to 350°F.

ii. Line a baking sheet with parchment paper

iii. Place the brie in the center of the sheet and bake for 10 minutes or until soft

iv. Cook butter and sugar in a frying pan on medium heat for 2 minutes or until the butter has melted

v. Stir in apple slices and cook for 5 minutes or until tender

vi. Transfer the brie from the baking sheet and arrange it on a decorative serving dish

vii. Pour the apple mixture on the Brie evenly and then drizzle some caramel sauce over top

viii. Serve with pretzel crisps

22. Brie on a baguette with pear and black pepper

Cooking Time: 15 minutes

Makes: 6

Ingredient List:

- 8 ounces of Brie cheese
- 1 box of water crackers
- 1 cored ripe pear cut in half and sliced thin
- ¼ tsp. of coarsely ground black pepper

wwwwwwwwwwwwwwwwwwwwwwwwwwwwwwwwwww

How to Cook:

i. Spread brie on crackers and place a slice of pear over top.

ii. Sprinkle with some pepper and serve

23. Grilled Pear and Brie Sandwich

Cooking Time: 10 minutes

Makes: 1

Ingredient List:

- 1 ounce softened butter
- 2 pieces of French bread, sliced thick
- 6 pieces of Brie cheese, sliced thin
- 12 thyme leaves
- ¼ tsp. cracked black pepper
- 6 pear slices
- A pinch of salt

wwwwwwwwwwwwwwwwwwwwwwwwwwwwwwwww

How to Cook:

i.   Butter each slice of French bread on one side

ii. Heat a large frying pan on medium heat and place the two pieces of bread butter side down in the pan

iii. Place cheese on one each slice of bread, then thyme, then black pepper

iv. On the second slice, add the pear slices to the Brie and then a small dash of salt

v.   Close the sandwich with a spatula and continue cooking for 3 minutes on each side or until the pear is tender and the cheese is melted

24. Honey Brie spread

Cooking Time: 5 minutes

Makes: 8

Ingredient List:

- 14-ounce wheel Brie cheese
- 10 ounces crescent roll dough
- 12 ounces honey
- 12 ounces pecans, halved

wwwwwwwwwwwwwwwwwwwwwwwwwwwwwwwwwwww

How to Cook:

i. Preheat the oven to 375°F.

ii. Remove the rind from the Brie

iii. Unroll the dough and then wrap it around the Brie, sealing the dough around the cheese by pressing with your fingers

iv. Put in a square baking dish and top with pecans and pour the honey over the top

v. Bake for 30 minutes or until cheese is soft and the exterior is golden brown

25. Brie Pizza

Cooking Time: 10 minutes

Makes: 16

Ingredient List:

- 8 1/2 ounces thinly sliced Brie
- 16 ounces almonds, sliced
- 14-ounce package of fully-baked pizza crust

wwwwwwwwwwwwwwwwwwwwwwwwwwwwwwwwwww

How to Cook:

i. Preheat an oven to 350°F

ii. Place pizza crust on a large pizza stone or baking sheet and cover evenly with the slices of Brie

iii. Sprinkle with almonds and bake for 10 minutes or until cheese has melted

26. Bacon Brie Panini

Cooking Time: 10 minutes

Makes: 2

Ingredient List:

- 1 ounce of room-temperature butter
- 2 slices Panini bread
- 1 tsp. Dijon
- 3 slices Brie
- 1 thinly sliced Fuji apple
- 4 cooked slices of bacon

wwwwwwwwwwwwwwwwwwwwwwwwwwwwwwwwwwwww

How to Cook:

i. Turn the Panini press on Medium-High

ii. Spread butter on 1 side of each slice of bread and then place the pieces butter side down on a plate. Layer mustard, cheese, apple, bacon, and then the other piece of bread.

iii. Put the sandwich in the press with the buttered sides facing out and press down for 3 minutes per side or until the bread reaches a light brown color and the cheese is melted

27. Brie Asparagus Casserole

Cooking Time: 10 minutes

Makes:6

Ingredient List:

- 12 ounces orecchiette pasta, uncooked
- 1 tsp. butter
- 1 trimmed bunch of asparagus, sliced in thirds
- 6 ounces heavy whipping cream
- A pinch of salt and black pepper
- 8 ounces of Brie cheese, cubed
- 2 ounces bread crumbs

wwwwwwwwwwwwwwwwwwwwwwwwwwwwwwwwww

How to Cook:

i. Preheat oven to 400°F.

ii. Next, you will need to cook the pasta in a large pot of boiling water for a period of 10 minutes or until it is al dente

iii. Drain and transfer to a casserole dish

iv. In a medium frying pan, melt butter on medium heat

v. Add asparagus and cook for 5 minutes or until slightly soft

vi. Place asparagus on the pasta in the casserole dish

vii. Pour the heavy cream over top and sprinkle with salt and pepper

viii. Place the Brie evenly over the top of the cream and then add bread crumbs

ix. Bake for 30 minutes or until cheese is melted

28. Spinach and Brie Linguine

Cooking Time: 15 minutes

Makes:4

Ingredient List:

- 8 ounces of linguine pasta, uncooked
- 4 halved slices of bacon
- 16 ounces of rinsed baby spinach, dried
- 1 minced clove garlic
- 2 ounces of Brie cheese, cut into cubes
- olive oil

wwwwwwwwwwwwwwwwwwwwwwwwwwwwwwwwwww

How to Cook:

i. Begin by cooking the linguine. To do this, you will add it to a pot of boiling water for 8 minutes or until it is al dente.

ii. Drain the noodles in a colander and then set aside

iii. In a large frying pan over medium heat, cook the bacon for 2 minutes per side or until crispy

iv. Remove the bacon and set it on a paper towel to drain, but leave the grease in the frying pan

v. Cook garlic in the grease until lightly browned, then add spinach and cook for 2 minutes or until wilted

vi. Remove the frying pan from heat, add pasta, brie, and olive oil and toss until cheese is melted and pasta is completely coated

29. Chicken Wellington with Brie

Cooking Time: 15 minutes

Makes: 4

Ingredient List:

- Cooking spray
- ½ ounce olive oil
- 32 ounces of thinly sliced boneless and skinless chicken breasts
- 1/3 ounce Creole seasoning
- 1 tsp. salt
- 1 tsp. black pepper, ground
- 2 thawed sheets of frozen puff pastry
- 4 crumbled slices of cooked bacon
- 4 ounces Brie, cut into 4 slices

wwwwwwwwwwwwwwwwwwwwwwwwwwwwwwwwwww

How to Cook:

i. Preheat oven to 400°F

ii. Lightly coat a baking sheet with cooking spray

iii. In a large frying pan on Medium heat, heat olive oil

iv. Sprinkle creole seasoning, salt, and pepper on the chicken and place in the heated oil for 2 minutes per side or until browned evenly

v. Roll the puff pastry sheets out and cut them in half

vi. Place 8 ounces of chicken breast on each pastry half, with 1 slice of crumbled bacon and 1 slice of Brie

vii. Fold the pastry over the chicken and close the seams by pressing them with your fingers

viii. Put each rolled chicken mixture on the baking sheet with the seams facing down

ix. Cook for 20 minutes or until the pastry is golden brown and the chicken is completely cooked through with no pink in the middle.

30. Brie Pasta

Cooking Time: 15 minutes

Makes:8

Ingredient List:

- 16 ounces of cubed Brie cheese
- 4 diced plum tomatoes
- 8 ounces basil, shredded
- 4 ounces olive oil
- 3 crushed cloves garlic
- 1/2 tsp. salt
- 1/4 tsp. black pepper, ground
- 24 ounces bow-tie pasta
- ½ ounce olive oil
- 1/3 ounce salt
- 2 ounces Parmesan cheese, grated

wwwwwwwwwwwwwwwwwwwwwwwwwwwwwwwwwww

How to Cook:

i. Combine Brie, tomatoes, basil, 4 ounces of oil, ½ tsp. of salt, and pepper in a large mixing bowl. Cover the bowl with plastic wrap and chill for 2 hours in the refrigerator

ii. Boil a large stock pot of water with ½ ounce of olive oil and 1/3 ounce of salt

iii. Cook pasta for 12 minutes or until al dente, then drain

iv. Transfer pasta to a large serving bowl and cover it with the tomato mixture and toss

v. Add parmesan cheese on top

Author's Afterthoughts

thank you
FOR YOUR ORDER

Practice makes perfect in the same way that expressing gratitude paves the way to success because it allows you to become surrounded by people who know how much you value them in your journey. I've been blessed to have a loving family, amazing friends, and beautiful readers like you who support me and push me to constantly improve by trying out my recipes!

I'm so grateful that I'd like to give back to you and all of my readers by asking what kind of content you'd like to see more of. Is it a book on a particular cuisine or cooking style? Would you like me to work on more weeknight recipes? I'm excited to know what your thoughts are so I can start brainstorming on my next cookbook! I read all of my replies, reviews, and suggestions, so don't hesitate to leave me a comment because I WILL get to it and put it to good use in my writing and cooking. `

Thanks a bunch!

Rola Oliver

About the Author

Cooking never really interested Rola until her family moved to Connecticut and the kids at her school began making fun of her because of her southern accent. From middle school all the way up to high school, Rola spent her afternoons at home. While life passed her by, her Nana was always in kitchen up to something delicious. Sometimes it would smell like onion, others of pie. Although Rola rarely left the sofa, her mind would wander to so many places with the smell of Nana's cooking. And when she ate, the flavors always surprised her!

Eventually, Nana was able to get Rola into the kitchen without saying a single word. The sounds of the kitchen knives and pans were a comforting feeling because they reminded her of Nana, her favorite person in the world.

At first, Rola spent up to 20 minutes chopping an onion… but fast forward twenty five years and Rola is now a celebrated southern cook in Connecticut! Nana isn't usually cooking anymore, but every now and then she still likes to pop in and watch her granddaughter at work. Together, they own a growing southern food joint, working hard to preserve traditions and authentic southern flavors.

Made in the USA
Las Vegas, NV
14 December 2024

14149402R00039